MINE'S A PINT

THE STORY OF
BRADFIELD BREWERY

First published in Great Britain in 2016 on behalf of:
Bradfield Brewery – www.bradfieldbrewery.com
Watt House Farm, High Bradfield, Sheffield, S6 6LG
Tel: 0114 285 1118

Published by:
RMC Media – www.rmcmedia.co.uk
6 Broadfield Court, Sheffield, S8 0XF
Tel: 0114 250 6300

Author: Adam Kay
Design: Richard Abbey
Proof-reader: Christopher Brierley

Printed and bound in Great Britain by:
CPI Colour Ltd – www.cpicolour.co.uk
108-110 Beddington Lane, Croydon, Surrey, CR0 4YY
Tel: 020 8688 7500

A CIP catalogue record for this book is available from the British Library.

ISBN: 978-1-907998-26-3

Mine's a
PINT

John Gill remembers the early days of Bradfield Brewery well. Back then, it was just him and his wife Susan, delivering everything by hand themselves. Thing is, it wasn't pints of beer they were selling in those days, but pints of milk.

At that time, most dairy farms had a milk round. Farmers would milk their cows, bottle the milk themselves, and then go off to sell it around the local villages. The milk John and Susan delivered came from Watt House Farm, owned by Susan's family – but the pair's own milk round experience was to be something of a bumpy ride...

John and Susan bought an old newspaper van to use for their deliveries. Perfect, they thought – until they realised the vehicle only had a driver's seat. The passenger side was empty, so that piles of papers could be stacked and delivered straight out through the door. The young couple had to improvise: when they took the van out for deliveries, John would drive... and Susan would sit beside him on a milk crate.

From those humble beginnings, the Gills have driven Watt House Farm to the height of success. As the home of Bradfield Brewery, it's now responsible for some of the finest real ales in the country.

In the South Yorkshire area, Bradfield Brewery's beers are as celebrated as they are popular, winning award after award and selling by the barrel-load. But they are enjoyed up and down the UK as well – a nationwide success story for a very local business.

From the start, Bradfield Brewery has been a family affair. The idea to set up a brewery in the first place came from John and Susan's son Richard, a beer lover who saw an opportunity to diversify the farm when milk prices took a tumble around 2004. Today he steers the business, together with his sister Lisa and John and Susan themselves. But the brewery is an extended family too, with loyal staff who have been with the Gills from the very beginning.

This book celebrates more than a decade of success – and to make it a proper celebration, also featured are some stunning recipes from Whitby's famous Magpie Café, seafood specialists and firm friends of the brewery.

This is the story of the farming family that swapped pints of milk for pints of beer. It's a story of hard work, dedication and, yes, the occasional cow. It's the story of Bradfield Brewery. Pour yourself a pint and read on...

Setting the
SCENE

Rolling fields in every direction, dry stone walls standing quaint and ancient and proud, the sunlight glittering over mirror-glass water... welcome to beautiful Bradfield.

The area from which Bradfield Brewery gets its name is home to some truly stunning scenery – and a fascinating history all of its own.

One of the largest parishes in England, Bradfield sits towards the north of Sheffield, within the Peak District National Park – which goes some way to accounting for its natural beauty. It covers an area of extensive moorland, used for agricultural purposes for many hundreds of years. It's also well known for its four reservoirs: Damflask, Dale Dyke, Strines and Agden.

The village itself is split into two divisions: Low Bradfield and High Bradfield. Much of Low Bradfield was devastated when the Dale Dyke Reservoir burst in 1864, causing the Great Sheffield Flood, one of the city's most infamous tragedies.

Bradfield Brewery's Watt House Farm is located in High Bradfield, an area known for its ancient buildings. Bailey Hill, the site of a Norman Motte-and-bailey castle, is a local landmark, as is St Nicholas Church, a Gothic structure dating back to the 1480s.

Beautiful and historic it may be, but Bradfield's exposed location regularly leaves it at the mercy of the elements, as John Gill explains...

"We get affected by bad weather quite a lot," he says. "We're often on the news. I remember one time the wind took out some of the overhead power lines. We had to rig something up temporarily using a tractor, because we were in the middle of milking cows at the time!"

Power problems aside, Bradfield is one of the most picturesque parts of the region – so there was never any doubt as to what the Gills were going to name their brewing venture. But the family also wanted to keep their farming heritage alive – so in the early days, the decision was made to advertise Bradfield Brewery's beers as 'Farmers Ales'.

"We thought it rolled off the tongue nicely: 'Have a pint of Farmers!'" says John. "It worked well, but perhaps a bit too well. I remember a chap telling me that he'd asked his brother if he'd tried Bradfield ale, to which the brother said he hadn't. But when he asked if his brother had tried Farmers ale, he said yes – he hadn't realised they were the same!"

These days, it's definitely Bradfield Brewery all the way – although the Farmers title is still used for the brewery's core range, such as Farmers Stout, Farmers Ale and so on. For the Gills, it's all about remembering your roots – and while today they may be champion beer makers, they were a proud farming family first.

"Bradfield is one of the most picturesque parts of the region — so there was never any doubt as to what the Gills were going to name their brewing venture."

Down on the
FARM

Head up to Watt House Farm today, and you'll see a busy, thriving, thoroughly modern brewery in full swing. From the shining brew tanks cooking up the next batch, to the onsite shop with bottles and kegs piled high, there's no doubting what the stock in trade is here.

Susan Gill sees it through different eyes. When she looks around the site, it's still the family farm she grew up on.

"When we started brewing, we put tarmac down around the barn which we'd converted into the brewery, but the rest of the farm still had the original surfacing," says Susan. "John used to point the tarmac out to visitors and say 'That's where the brewing stops and the farming starts.' When we tarmacked the rest of it, that tale had to stop!"

Of course, Susan never expected to be brewing beer in the first place – as a proud farmer's daughter, she thought she'd be milking cows all her life. Thanks to her and her family, Watt House Farm has been given a new lease of life.

Records show that there had been agricultural buildings on the site of Watt House Farm for many years, but the current structures only date back as far as 1908. Why? Because of an ambitious gentleman farmer named Henry Sanderson.

Mr Sanderson was a widower who lived with his mother-in-law. She owned some of the farms in the Bradfield area, for which he acted as bailiff. When she died in 1906, she left him the equivalent of £2million in today's money. Henry knew exactly what he wanted to do with his windfall: to knock down Watt House Farm and rebuild it from scratch as a model farm.

"I think we're reaping the benefits of that now," says John Gill. "Some of the buildings at the bottom are completely tiled out, the quality of everything, even the wood used, was second to none... there was no expense spared."

Mr Sanderson passed away in the early 1920s, and with no children of his own to leave the farm to, it passed to his three nieces. The trio had no interest in farming, so they rented it out to the Plant family. When the Plants decided to move to the nearby village of Oughtibridge instead, Watt House Farm was taken over, on 16th May 1944, by Susan's grandfather. Many years later, that date was to become significant for the Hagues' granddaughter Susan – it was the day she was to become Mrs Susan Gill.

John Gill wasn't a farmer's son, but through happenstance he fell in love with farming – and also a farmer's daughter.

John's introduction to farm life came through his older sister. She married into a farming family, and young John, ten years old at the time, would help his new brother-in-law with his farming duties and milk rounds.

"I used to love it," says John. "All my holidays and weekends were spent on the farm. More than anything else, it got me some pocket money!"

By the time John was ready to leave school, farming was an all-consuming passion – but even though it had made him his pocket money, he didn't feel agriculture was a viable career option. Instead, John became a motor mechanic – something that made him the envy of all his friends when he was able to buy and run his own moped, and later, at the age of 17, his own car.

It was around this time that John was approached by one of the girls from his old school; in typical teenage fashion, she told him "My mate fancies you!" That mate turned out to be Susan, who John soon began dating – and who he was delighted to discover was a farmer's daughter. Destiny? Fate? For John, it was simply meant to be.

By 1977, John had left the motor industry and was running his own milk round in the early mornings, then working at Watt House Farm for Susan's father straight afterwards. Susan had her own milk round as well – and John was happy when they combined their duties to become colleagues rather than rivals...

"I always tell people I married Susan for her milk round," he laughs, "Her customers were next door to mine!"

Sure enough, the pair were married, on 16th May 1981 – 37 years to the day after Susan's family took over Watt House Farm. John moved in with his in-laws, and soon the newlyweds were blessed with a family of their own: son Richard in 1983, and daughter Lisa in 1985.

Susan's father Stan was very much the head of his family and the boss of the farm – but from the very beginning of their relationship, John and Susan had largely taken over the day-to-day running of the place. The couple's energy and keen enthusiasm for farming didn't go unnoticed.

"From an early age we were calling the shots, running the farm as we wanted," says John. "As time went on we had more and more influence on the way things were done – putting in a parlour with cubicles for the cows, for example."

With Stan taking a backseat, John and Susan eventually persuaded him to let them take control on a more formal basis. In 1988, they took on full responsibility for the farm's dairy cows. Watt House Farm had entered a new era.

Building
BLOCKS

John Gill has always had a passion for vehicles. Maybe it comes from his days as a motor mechanic, but if it's got wheels and an engine, John likes it.

One of Watt House Farm's big old barns, down the hill from the brewery, is now used to store bottles, casks and kegs of beer – but it's also home to John's automotive collection...

"I've got some lovely old tractors, and a lightweight Land Rover," he says. "There's also a Mercedes-Benz Unimog truck, which I've driven through the village before – people don't half move out of your way when they see that coming!"

Watt House Farm is a brewery now, of course, but beer wasn't the family's first foray into diversification – that came much earlier, thanks to petrolhead John...

"I'd always seen these little machines around – a sort of mini tractor," he says. "They were called Bobcats. Because we only had small spaces in between our buildings at the farm, I thought they might be useful for moving things around, so we bought one."

Spotting a business opportunity, John soon began hiring his services with the Bobcat out to local building sites and other construction projects. Ironically, one of the first jobs he worked on was the Whitbread Brewery in Sheffield.

This was 1990, and John's new enterprise was bringing in extra money, which was all ploughed back into the farm. But this increased workload was becoming a struggle for John and Susan, not least because of the two young children they were raising at the same time. Thankfully, help was to land at the Gills' doorstep – or rather run past it...

"I had a newspaper round, and John saw me running around delivering the papers," says Pete Jackson. "He asked me how much I was getting paid, which was about three pounds a week. He said: 'I'll give you two pounds a day if you run round like that delivering milk for me instead!'"

For Pete, a young teenager at the time, that was an offer he couldn't refuse – and he's been part of the Watt House Farm team ever since.

"At first I helped with taking the milk out, then on Saturdays I came back to wash the bottles and bottle the milk," says Pete. "Then I started doing bits and pieces of work helping out on the farm – I'd come during the school holidays. Then I took over with the Bobcat, and it all snowballed from there really."

With Pete's loyal help, and another string to the family's bow in the Bobcat business, things were going well for the Gills. The next milestone was to come in March 1991, when the family, who had moved out to live at nearby Stannington, persuaded Susan's parents to take full retirement. The Hagues moved out, and the Gills were back at Watt House Farm.

Pete Jackson

Although John and Susan were now running things full-time, there was always a niggling annoyance at the back of their minds: the fact that the farm wasn't truly theirs. Like so many of the agricultural businesses in the area, Watt House Farm was actually a rented property, owned by the council. After years of asking if there was the chance to purchase it privately, a letter arrived out of the blue informing the Gills the farm was for sale. The family snatched the opportunity with both hands, and by 1998 the deal was done. For John and Susan, it was another momentous occasion.

All was well in the Gills' world – but the world around them was changing, and events were to cause their lives to take a different course. The rise of supermarket shopping had led to a decline in the popularity of milk rounds – now, people were simply getting their milk elsewhere. As dairy farmers, John and Susan had other options – but making a decision wasn't easy...

"At that time you had to buy a licence to make milk, called a milk quota, based on how many cows you milked and how much milk you made," says John. "We sold our milk round and bought some extra cows to make our money that way instead. That was a big thing for us – our milk round days over. I'd done it since I was ten, and Susan since she could walk!"

It was a bittersweet moment for the pair. But their decision turned out to be the right one: in the years that followed, the prices of milk rounds in the area – and indeed around the country – fell into rapid decline.

Ever resourceful, the Gills built up their dairy herd, buying more and more cows from local farmers who were looking to sell; at their peak, there were a herd of 120 dairy cows and 80 young stock at Watt House Farm. Then came the 2001 foot and mouth outbreak.

The sudden spread of infectious disease decimated the UK's farming industry; by the end of the crisis, it was estimated that 10 million sheep and cattle had been killed. When the industry began to recover, John hoped Watt House Farm's fortunes would improve, but it wasn't to be.

"We were always hoping for that extra penny or two a litre – we didn't owe anybody anything, but we were just treading water," says John. "Looking back, the only thing that was really bringing any money in was the Bobcat machines."

By now, the Gills had two Bobcats, which were booked out solidly with work at brickyards and so on. But when nearby brickyards began closing down, John started to get worried. With the difficulties in the farming industry and the possibility that their plant hire business could soon slow down, the family had to weigh up other options.

Whatever was decided, it was clear that Watt House Farm would need to be transformed. The family could never have known it, but those Bobcat diggers were to about become more useful than ever before. Thank goodness for John and his vehicle collection...

You're an 18-year-old-lad. You live in the north of England. Chances are you like your beer.

That was certainly the case for Richard Gill. But unlike many his age, Richard didn't see beer as simply something to drink and get drunk on.

"On a Friday, once we'd done milking, we'd get washed and changed and go down the real ale pubs," says Richard. "We always found ourselves looking for something different from the run-of-the-mill beers."

Unsatisfied by what was on offer at his local watering holes, Richard's thoughts turned to making beer of his own. His inspiration? His dad.

"I'd always dabbled at home-brewing – making a bit of wine or beer," says John Gill. "I was never too serious – I used to buy a beer kit, which just involves pouring things together and leaving the mixture in a cupboard for a fortnight. But Richard started to take it quite seriously."

Richard remembered his dad's attempts at home-brewing and decided to give it a go himself – but ultimately, he was disappointed by the results. A little light research led him to a book that was to broaden his horizons – and eventually change the family's fortunes...

"The first book I got was 'Brewing Beers Like Those You Buy' by Dave Line, which had a few beer recipes in – it basically all started from there," says Richard. "It told you about putting a proper brew kit together, with a mash tun and boiler, and explained the process behind it all."

Richard bought more and more books, teaching himself the science behind great beer – how the different ingredients reacted against each other, how to make beer taste better and so on. Before long, he was confident enough to test his wares on a wider audience...

"It was Lisa's 18th birthday, and Richard said he wanted to brew all the beers for the party," says John. "He linked them all up on these five-gallon tubs into hand-pulls which we'd installed. They tasted bloody good, not like your usual home-brewed stuff – it was nice beer."

Richard's hobby was keeping him busy – but at the same time the Gills were in a period of uncertainty. With the family's milking business just breaking even, and worries about their machine hire enterprise, they were keen to find something else to help ease the pressure. John's first thought was his passion for all things petrol.

"I'd taken my lorry test at age 26, so I could have worked for somebody else as a lorry driver if I wanted," he says. "But then I would have been away from home all the time – so although I could do it, it didn't appeal to me."

Another hobby was suggested as a business idea: garden furniture. As a family with a lifetime of experience in manual labour, the Gills were good with their hands – and when they installed a patio at their home, they built all the furniture for it themselves. But again, even though this was something they could have done without blinking, the problem was whether or not they wanted to. After some soul-searching, the answer was no.

"I couldn't really see myself in an apron all day making furniture," says John. "It was another option, but it didn't grab me." Meanwhile, Richard's home-brew hobby was still in full swing – but such was the scale of his brewing, it had started to become something of an irritation...

"Saturdays and Sundays were brewing days – I had all my equipment set up on the kitchen table," he says. "Mum used to pull her hair out because the steam from the kit made all the wallpaper come down!"

At the time, the Gills – now milking more cows than ever before – had installed a new milk tank in one of the old farm buildings to cope with their extra output. As it turned out, the tank didn't fill up the space it was intended to.

John and Susan had a lightbulb moment: why not install a small, permanent brew kit in the space, to allow Richard to carry on his hobby and get him out from under his mother's feet? While the idea was being mulled over, Richard had a lightbulb moment of his own...

"I knew we needed to diversify to make some more money," he says. "I remember running in to see my dad: 'What about a microbrewery?'"

A microbrewery? On a farm? It was just crazy enough to work...

All hands on
DECK

When you've dedicated your entire life to a single cause, how do you leave it behind and move on? Where do you find the strength to start anew when you can no longer do the only work you've ever known?

That was the challenge now facing the Gill family. Farming – the industry John, Susan and their children had been involved in since they could walk – would have to be swept to the sidelines. A new path had to be taken – and that was a daunting prospect. They needed help.

"At that time, you could apply for a grant from the government to get an advisor to visit you and give some general advice," says John Gill. "We took them up on that, and this chap came to us: Chris Franklin."

Chris was a business advisor with Business Link South Yorkshire, advising farm owners in the region about their diversification options. His help would prove instrumental to the future of Watt House Farm.

At the family's first meeting with Chris, they explained to him the ideas they'd been having: lorry driving, furniture making. But it was a throwaway comment from Chris which spurred the family on to consider other options...

"The meeting went pretty well, but as Chris was walking out of the door he said 'Whatever you decide to do, make sure it's something you really enjoy,'" says John. "That stuck in our minds!"

With their eyes opened to other possibilities, the Gills went away for a rethink – and landed on a winner with the suggestion of a brewery. Or so they thought. At the time, Chris Franklin saw it differently...

"My first reaction was to laugh!" says Chris. "Having been a business advisor to dozens if not hundreds of farmers around the area, I'd heard some pretty whacky ideas. Their suggestion of a brewery really did seem to come a bit out of leftfield – from talking about building benches and things, suddenly this seemed very, very different."

Despite his initial scepticism, Chris agreed to have a second meeting with the family to hear them out.

"It was very clear that they were extremely committed to the idea and weren't going to be put off by any knock-backs they might have," he says. "One of the options then was to start looking at some grant funding."

From Chris's advice, the family began the process of applying for a grant through the European Agricultural Guarantee Fund. But to be successful, the Gills needed to prove theirs was a viable business idea – they were, after all, a farm that wanted to become a brewery. Chris suggested some market research was needed – and when John found out what that involved, he was the first to volunteer...

"Together with Chris, we came up with a short questionnaire to find out if people would be interested in buying any beer we produced," says John. "Chris told us to visit 50 pubs to get their feedback. It's a hard job, but somebody had to do it...!"

Martyrs for the job they may have been, but the Gills got a great response from their research. With the information gathered, they were able to compile a business plan and send it off to the authorities. There followed a tense wait – one which lasted almost 12 months. Then, in early 2004, came the moment of truth: confirmation that the application had been accepted and the grant approved. Now it was all systems go.

"One of the first jobs we had to do was digging out the floor of the building we were going to use for brewing, because it was sloping," says John. "There was about 200 tonnes of muck to be moved. Me and Richard did most of the graft, and Pete Jackson would help when he wasn't working on a site with our Bobcat business."

Indeed, an old friend from the early days of John's Bobcat business was to lend a helping hand as the brewery began to take shape.

"Alan Smith used to work for a building firm which had hired one of our machines – I think the first thing he ever did when I met him was put a bacon butty in my hand, so I got on with him straight away!" laughs John. "He knew a lot about building regulations, so he would come up on a weekend and make sure we'd done everything we needed to."

Before too long, the family had a place in which to brew beer; now they just needed something to brew it on. The search for equipment began – but it soon hit a serious snag.

As proud patriots, the Gills were keen that everything they would use to make their beer would be British – the ingredients, the equipment, all of it. With this credo in mind, John commissioned an English company to create their custom brewing kit. Months

of expectation and excitement followed, but when John and Richard went to inspect the kit, the work hadn't been started. With the deal broken, the family were back to square one.

John in particular was at a low ebb, not knowing where to turn – but this time, a solution was to present itself. The family received an offer for a new brewing kit, built in that bastion of engineering, Germany.

"It sounds posh, but the company did actually have an office in Sheffield," John chuckles. "We didn't have to learn to speak German or anything like that!"

In fact, the equipment they'd been offered was revolutionary in the brewing world. Typical brewing kits are comprised of three vessels: a mash tun, a hot liquor tank and a 'copper', in which all the ingredients are finally boiled together to produce the beer. The system offered to the Gills was made up of just two vessels, with the mash tun and hot liquor tank combined into one – German efficiency at its finest.

After a brief back and forth – the family had planned that their farm-based brewery would have a very traditional look, and this equipment was practically space-age – the purchase went ahead. All the pieces of the jigsaw were finally in place.

"I know there were some pretty dark days – I could see that John was getting to the point of despair, almost, with the trials and tribulations of getting the equipment," says Chris Franklin. "But they stuck with it. I think they did a fabulous job in terms of creating the brewery, and the business. From what I've seen, they've just gone from strength to strength ever since."

Watt House Farm was still – and will always be – a farm. But now, with a dedicated building and a state-of-the-art brewing kit within, it was a brewery as well. And on 26th April 2005, Bradfield Brewery reached its first milestone on the road to success: the first brew.

Brewing up a
STORM

Fortune has played a big part in the success of Bradfield Brewery. Perhaps Watt House Farm is surrounded by four-leaf clovers.

Of course, the main reason for that success is the hard work of the Gills and their loyal staff. But there have also been moments where Lady Luck has smiled and things have fallen into place at exactly the right time.

One such moment was the arrival of head brewer Paul Ward, as John Gill explains.

"Richard kept getting an email asking if we were looking for a head brewer," says John. "We were planning to manage everything ourselves – brew the beer, milk the cows, do the deliveries. We said: 'We're alright on our own, us!'"

Nevertheless, Paul had some spare tickets to the Great British Beer Festival in London, and invited the Gill family along with him.

"While we were there, Paul won the Supreme Champion Beer of Britain award for a beer he'd brewed," says John. "I offered him the job on the train ride home!"

Sheffield born and bred, Paul had never planned on a career in brewing. But after graduating from university, he took a job in the office of a brewery in his hometown – and soon found himself drawn to 'the other side'.

"I started doing two days a week in the brewery, and the rest in the office," Paul explains. "But they always say once you get into brewing, you never get out!"

Paul fell immediately in love with the art of beer-making, and worked his way up to become head brewer, before taking on a consultancy role at another local brewery. When John Gill offered him the position at Bradfield Brewery, Paul saw the opportunity to indulge his passion further, and help build a new brewing business from the ground up.

"Brewing is a different world – it's like being a mad chef, creating new recipes for beer," he says. "The satisfaction comes when you're sat in the pub and everyone is drinking your beer. You think: 'I've done that.'"

They may not have been looking for a head brewer at the time, but with Paul on board the Gills now had all the elements in place to begin their new venture in earnest.

"Originally, we were going to let Richard do the brewing full-time, and he would have built it up into a success, because he's very good like that – everything he does, he follows through to the end," says Susan Gill. "But because Paul had already got a lot of knowledge on commercial brewing, I think that helped us."

From the outset, Richard and Paul developed a partnership which continues to produce winning results to this day. But at the very beginning, the big question was: what to brew?

COLD WATER TEMP

°C

OUT

SP ALM   ALM 1 2

E5CSV

omron

"We had come up with a few ideas," says Richard. "We wanted to keep our beer simple and traditional, so that people knew what they were drinking."

"When I came here, I said to the family: 'You can either make beer that wins loads of awards, or beer that people want to drink,'" says Paul. "Don't get me wrong, we have won quite a lot of awards since then – but we just wanted people to have a pint of our beer and then say 'I'll have another one!'"

With their theme of tradition in mind, Paul, Richard and the family decided on a core range of three beers as their first brews: a bitter, a stout and a pale ale. It was hoped these time-honoured classics would appeal to a wide range of beer drinkers – and so it has proved, with all three still being among Bradfield Brewery's most popular offerings.

"Getting that first brew in was a big moment," says Richard. The bitter was brewed on 26th April 2005, with the stout and pale ale following shortly after. "We'd been waiting so long to get started, to actually see it all working and coming together was really special."

Now, finally, Bradfield Brewery had produced its first beer. The next task was to sell it. As John explains, this was uncharted territory for the Gills.

"At that time, we'd come from producing milk that was taken away in a tanker, with no involvement from us about selling it or even getting a price for it," says John, referring to the milk dairy quota system. "Suddenly we'd got this product to sell."

As always, the family banded together, each of them taking it upon themselves to learn the ropes when it came to sales. For those first nervous months, it was a case of trial of error.

"From day one, we were members of SIBA – the Small Independent Brewers Association," says John. "That was a big thing, because you can get orders into tied pubs through them."

"We also got Beer Matters, the newsletter of CAMRA – the Campaign for Real Ale," John says. "We'd find out which pubs were freehouses and give them a ring to see if they'd be interested in taking the beer. We learnt on our feet."

As the new kids on the brewing block, and with their no-nonsense approach, it wasn't long before orders for the Gills' beer began trickling in. For the family, this was vindication that their hard work was paying off – but even they were surprised by how quickly word started to spread.

"I'd got this belief that when we started brewing, everyone in Sheffield would buy our beer, and that's as far as we'd go," says John. "But we'd only been going a month or so when we got an order in from Alfreton in Derbyshire. I thought, 'Bloody hell, that's a long way to go with some beer!'"

Now Alfreton is one of Bradfield Brewery's doorstop deliveries. As the business has grown in the intervening years, the brewery's distribution network has stretched as far north as Newcastle and as far south as Peterborough, and coast to coast from Blackpool to Bridlington. For the first 12 months or so, John and Susan did the majority of the deliveries themselves; now Bradfield Brewery commands a fleet of lorries and vans, taking their beer the length and breadth of the country.

Back in those early days, and with demand increasing day by day, the Gills also focused on selling their beer a little closer to home.

"We had a little shop onsite as soon as we got the licence for it," says Susan Gill. "Even at the very beginning, we'd get people coming in every day to buy the beer."

After the hardships in getting the business set up in the first place – the agonising wait to find out if grant funding had been approved, the setback with the uncompleted brewing equipment – things were now off to a flying start. But the Gills soon came to the realisation that they would need to sell something else as well...

"For the first few months, we were doing everything ourselves – sales, delivery, brewing, the lot," says John. "And at the same time, we were still milking."

"Brewing was a scary new world for us – we'd hung everything onto it, and I don't know what we'd have done if it hadn't been a success," he says. "At the time, we were getting 15.5 pence per litre for the milk we produced, and we worked out that it was costing us 20 pence to produce. We didn't want the brewery to subsidise the cows."

"We had to make the heartfelt decision to sell them," John continues. "In August a chap came over from Huddersfield to look at the cows, gave us a price for the lot, and that was it – off he went."

"It was one of the biggest decisions me and Susan have ever made," says John. "Despite the fact that we weren't earning any money from the dairy business at that point, it was what we knew – we could go into a parlour blindfolded and start milking cows!"

"Suddenly, we didn't have to wake up in a morning and worry about whose turn it was to milk!" he laughs. "Those first weekends without cows were very sad and strange, and especially that first Christmas. I wouldn't like to go back to that lifestyle now, but it seemed really, really weird to us at the time."

It was the closing of another chapter in the life of Watt House Farm – but the start of a brand new one. From here on out, there was no looking back.

Gentlemen (and ladies!) prefer
BLONDE

BRADFIELD
BREWERY

In 2014, no less an institution than the New York Times quoted Sheffield as being Britain's best beer city. Our friends across the pond have a point.

There are more breweries per capita in the Sheffield City Region than anywhere else outside London. The UK's craft beer revolution is said to have originated in the Steel City, thanks to the pubs and microbreweries of the Kelham Island area. Perhaps there's something in the water – with the city being built on the confluence of five rivers, there's plenty of it around to brew with.

Clearly, Sheffielders are spoiled for choice when it comes to ale – so you might imagine picking a favourite would prove difficult. But on the annual lists of the city's best-selling beers produced by Sheffield CAMRA, one variety is always at or very near the top: Bradfield Brewery's Farmers Blonde.

There are thousands of blonde beers, made by breweries around the world. But walk into any Sheffield pub worth its salt and ask for "a pint of blonde," and chances are you'll be handed a glass with a Bradfield Brewery logo printed on the side.

Pale in colour and refreshing to the taste, with aromas of citrus and summer fruit, it's not hard to see why this easy-drinking ale has become a Sheffield favourite. First brewed only a few months into Bradfield Brewery's existence, it's been popular from the start. But what was the inspiration behind the bestseller?

"One of the big pub chains held a competition for breweries in South Yorkshire, and we were invited to brew two different beers – a dark one and a light one," says John Gill. "The actual competition withered away, but we still made the beers."

The light one was, obviously, Farmers Blonde. The other one was Farmers Brown Cow, a rich chestnut-coloured ale. As the first beers produced outside the core range of three, they represented another milestone for the brewery. Both have been in permanent production ever since.

When the Gills decided to take the plunge and move into brewing beer, they knew they would need to spread the word as quickly and effectively as possible. But with such a unique story and a clear idea about the brand, getting the message across was never going to be a problem.

As well as the money they had secured to help build the brewery in the first place, the family were able to get some funding towards marketing their new business. They were introduced to a design firm who were tasked with coming up with a branding concept – but when the first drafts came back, the Gills were less than impressed.

"So we went back to how we make most of our decisions," says John, "Which is together as a family, sat round the kitchen table, saying 'What do you think of this?'"

For any business, and particularly a brand new one, the logo is all-important. Fortunately, the Gills had a firm idea.

"We wanted to use a millstone," says John. "That's what brewers used to use to grind their malt in days gone by. Then we wanted some hops, one of the main ingredients in beer, along the bottom of the logo."

The millstone was of course traditionally used for grinding grains and animal feed on farms – so for Bradfield Brewery, it was doubly relevant. John and Richard took their bright idea to a printing company in Sheffield.

"They came out with a rough drawing, and it was just what we wanted," says John. "It was something that said 'Bradfield Brewery' without needing to do a lot of reading!"

This was especially important to John. Having always struggled with reading and writing at school, he discovered later in life that he was actually dyslexic.

"Because of that, shapes mean a lot to me," he explains. "When we were setting up the brewery and going around pubs for research, I'd end up pointing at the pump clips rather than reading what was written on them."

John was adamant, then, that the Gills would use a distinctive pump clip shape for their beers. The idea was that in a pub, even if you were on the other side of the bar and only able to see the reverse of the clip rather than the design on the front, you would still be able to tell which one was a Bradfield Brewery beer. The version the family decided on, with the millstone logo at the top, is instantly recognisable.

The Gills felt it was crucial that Bradfield Brewery's identity should reflect the family's farming background. The millstone logo was part of this, but for the pump clip design of their first three beers – Bitter, Pale Ale and Stout – another agricultural item was added: a tractor. The original design has been updated in the years since, but a tractor is still used to represent all three brews, a reminder of the history of Watt House Farm.

With those first three beers, the aim was to keep things simple and traditional – including the titles. But when it came to naming their next brews, the Gills again looked to their farming roots for inspiration.

"What we wanted to do as a theme was name the beers after breeds of cow," says John. "Blonde is named after the Blonde d'Aquitaine breed, and Brown Cow is named after the Swiss Brown."

With five core beers established, what next? Brew more, of course! From the earliest days, Bradfield Brewery has produced a range of 'specials' to tie in with particular occasions and events. The first, in October of that first year, was Jack O'Lantern, brewed to commemorate Halloween. Since then, there have been beers to celebrate World Cups, festivals, St George's Day and many more besides. Again, these are often titled after breeds of cow – the regular St Patrick's Day brew is named Irish Dexter, for example.

For all the many specials produced over the years, however, one has eclipsed all others in popularity: Belgian Blue.

"I wanted to do a Christmas beer, but I also wanted to do a blue beer," explains Paul Ward. "I like to do things that make people go 'wow!'"

As Paul says, the thing that makes this special brew particularly special is its unique colour. The berry extract used in its production gives a slight blue tint to the head – and while it might be unusual to look at, its fruity taste is perfect for the festive season. And yes, the Belgian Blue is a breed of cow!

"We release it at the beginning of November, and people just go crazy for it," says Lisa Moat. "We once had somebody tweeting to say that he was the first person, other than us, to have a pint of Belgian Blue at that year's official launch – that was his claim to fame!"

Belgian Blue was actually brewed for Bradfield Brewery's first Christmas – a fitting way to end an incredibly productive first year. And just as Belgian Blue would grow and grow in popularity from that point onwards, so the brewery would become bigger than the Gills could ever have imagined.

Pulling
POWER

"For a good while, we used to go to bed thinking 'What if people don't like the beer? What if it doesn't sell?'"

It's understandable that Susan Gill was nervous – but she needn't have worried. Bradfield Brewery had got off to a flying start.

Word had spread rapidly about 'the farmers who brew beer', and their novel new venture had attracted much attention. With the launch of their special brews, particularly Farmers Blonde, they'd also gained an immediate army of fans.

Despite its speedy growth, however, this was still a fledgling business – and the Gills were heavily involved in every day-to-day task. By this time, John and Susan's daughter Lisa, who had studied catering at college and had been working in local pubs, came back to join the family business full-time. Lisa and Susan took on responsibility for the day-to-day running of the office and making the odd delivery – and they had their share of laughs along the way.

"On one occasion, we delivered to a wedding that was being held in the couple's home," says Susan. "It was summertime, and the groomsmen were all wearing cream-coloured suits."

"We had to roll the casks down the garden to where the beer was being served, and one of the men asked us to 'tap it in' for them – to set it up ready for drinking," she says. "Lisa tapped it in gently, but the beer shot out and went all over him!"

Over the next couple of years, Bradfield Brewery's sales went steadily upwards. Their ales travelled further and further, being stocked by pubs and retailers across the country, and winning more new fans along the way. But the Gill family aren't ones to rest on their laurels. By 2008, they were keen to take the brewery to the next step.

"I remember Richard saying 'We ought to have a pub of our own!'" says John. "The first pub we'd ever delivered to was the Nags Head Inn, literally down the road from our farm in Bradfield. Then when we were looking to buy one, we heard that the landlord there wanted to come out because he and his wife were expecting a child..."

The Bradfield Brewery journey had been filled with fortuitous moments, and here was the latest: the first pub to ever take Bradfield Brewery's beer would later be owned by... Bradfield Brewery! But once again, getting to that point wasn't going to be all plain sailing...

"The Nags Head was owned by one of the large pub chains, and they were half-thinking of selling it, so we approached them," says John. "We actually took it over on 08/08/08, the day the Olympics started in Beijing. But we were only renting it at the time, with what I thought was a clear understanding that we were going to get a deal worked out and buy it from them."

Unfortunately things didn't turn out to be so simple. The retailer actually placed the pub back on the open market – even going so far as to put up 'For Sale' signs in the forecourt. Fortunately, after some tough negotiating, the Gills were able to reach an agreement – and in January 2009, the Nags Head officially became theirs.

"The first job we did was completely redecorate it," says John. "We shut on the Sunday night about 11 o'clock, and worked right through the night with as many people as we could. We got it reopened at Monday teatime. Tiring, but fun!"

"I also remember, though, it was bloody cold at that time of year," John laughs. "We'd treated the bar with a lacquer and it absolutely stunk, so we had to have all the windows and doors open. We were freezing!"

Since taking over the Nags Head, the Gill children had spent time living at the pub – first Lisa and her partner (later husband) James, then Richard and his wife Josie. But the family all contributed to the running of their new venture, juggling it with their duties at the brewery. These days, landlady Megan Packham is at the helm, and the Nags Head has continued to go from strength to strength.

"When we first went in, we had three or four of our own beers on at £1.80 a pint, at the time," says Richard. "It was a bit of a no-brainer for the customers as to what they were going to drink. We got all the locals converted that way!"

For Richard, that was the secret to the pub's success. The Nags Head is very much still a friendly and welcoming local pub, but under the Gills' stewardship it has grown busier than ever before.

People know they can go in the Nags and get a decent pint at a decent price," he says. "And because it's busy, they know there's going to be somebody in there they can talk to, rather than a big empty pub that's selling beer at three or four pounds a pint."

Keeping things traditional is at the core of everything Bradfield Brewery do – and the same applies to the Nags Head.

"Right from day one I said, 'If we're having a pub, we need to serve real chips,' – I hate when you go for a meal somewhere and you get oven chips," says John. "It's important to keep things simple – you can't go wrong with a pie and a pint!"

By 2011, just six short years after the formation of the brewery, business was booming. With demand for beer coming from all corners of the UK, and a thriving pub in the shape of the Nags Head, the Gills' only problem was keeping on top of it all – admittedly a very nice problem to have.

With demand beginning to outstrip supply, however, it was time to take things to the next level. Bradfield Brewery was expanding.

"The Nags Head is very much still a friendly and welcoming local pub, but under the Gills' stewardship it has grown busier than ever before."

"In brewing, you work on what they call 'brewer's barrels' – one barrel is 36 gallons," says John. "Our original brew kit was a ten-barrel kit, so 360 gallons."

But as the business had grown, that was no longer enough. The Gills got back in touch with the manufacturer of their original brewing equipment in Germany to discuss their options – and came up with a plan for some brand new custom-built kit.

"The one we have now is a 40-barrel kit, so 1,440 gallons," explains John. "Putting it down to pints, you're looking at roughly 11,500 pints every time we brew."

It was a huge leap forward, but one that was very necessary. In order to accommodate the giant new brew tanks, though, the brewery itself needed to be bigger. Time to dig out the diggers again...

"When the brewery expanded, there was a mezzanine floor in the building which we'd built in," says Pete Jackson. "That had to be dismantled, and we did all that ourselves. The problem is that when we build things, we built them right – if a wall needs to be one foot thick, we'll make it two foot thick just to be sure. So when it comes to taking it down, it's twice as hard!"

"Even when we were putting the new kit in, the manufacturer plumbed it, but we actually put the tanks in," Pete continues. "So it really is self-built."

The 'new' brewery reopened in 2011. This was a year of dual celebration for the Gills – one that warranted a brush with celebrity...

"Our beer had been put on sale in the House of Commons," says John, still delighted at the memory of the honour. "When that happens, they give you a plaque. Because he was a Sheffield MP, it was arranged that Nick Clegg would come to present it to us."

John was keen that the then-deputy prime minister perform another duty during his visit as well...

"I thought that while he was coming up, he could officially open the new brewery!" John laughs. "He cut the ribbon for us – it was a great day."

A new Bradfield Brewery, now with the seal of approval from Westminster... it was a far cry from those humble beginnings, making beer in a homebrew kit on the kitchen table. Despite the raised profile, however, the attitude was the same as it had been at the start: a farming family, making something they loved from their Bradfield home. Bradfield was still at the heart of everything they did – and in a few short years, the Gills would find themselves in the middle of the biggest event in the area's history.

On yer
BIKE

TDF
KOM
CLIMB
2

CAT 4 CLIMB
940 m
AV GRADIENT: 9.9%

Côte de Bradfield
350 m

ude • 84 m
nit • 0.9 km

ad. • 19%   Ave. grad. • 9.2%

Cycle Yorkshire inmotion! Sheffield City Council

It is beautiful. It is serene. In parts, it appears unchanged through hundreds and hundreds of years.

The village of Bradfield is all these things and more – but it is not generally regarded as a focal point of international sport. But for one summer's day in 2014, that's exactly what it became.

Yes, this was the day when the Tour de France came to town. And right in the thick of it all was Bradfield Brewery.

"It was crazy – I've never seen anything like it in my life!" says Lisa Moat. "It was a bit stressful at the time though."

There was fevered excitement throughout Yorkshire when it was announced that Stages 1 and 2 of the famous cycling contest would pass through the county. And when it was revealed that one of the biggest spectator events on the planet would be coming to Bradfield, the mood was one of joyous disbelief.

"I'm not big into cycling, but I knew this was going to be special," says John Gill. "A meeting was held in the village hall which we attended. We knew we'd be doing something as part of it, but we didn't realise as to what scale. I think as the weeks went on it dawned on us just how big it was going to be."

With thousands expected to flock to the area and a carnival-like atmosphere predicted, the village wanted to pull out all the stops. Working with a local events company, Bradfield Brewery made plans to organise a beer festival to keep spectators suitably refreshed...

"We provided the field, and another field further away for camping – and arranged the beers of course," says John. "The Rotherham branch of CAMRA gave us a lot of help. I think we had ten of our on beers on, and 40 other beers and ciders."

"That sounds simple enough, but it was far from it!" he laughs. "We had to provide parking for cars, a safe passage from the festival field to the campsite, security guards on the gates... it was a nightmare to run, but at the end of the day it was so worth it."

Never ones to miss an opportunity, the Gills brewed a special beer as a tie-in to the Tour. Their Yellow Jersey ale was a light, refreshing brew, the ideal accompaniment to a summer's day spent watching top cyclists whizz by. A new logo was even devised, with the distinctive millstone replaced with a bicycle wheel.

Things didn't go entirely without a hitch, however.

"The council had provided us with toilets and fencing, but the day before the race an inspector came round to check on everything, and he said it wasn't up to scratch – we thought everything had already been approved," says John. "The council sent some more provisions, but just as we were frantically trying to get it all sorted the weather changed and it started to rain!"

Fortunately, everything worked out in the end. On the day of the race, Sunday 6th July 2014, the rolling roads of Bradfield were lined with cheering crowds, waving flags and soaking up the spectacle. To top it off, the sun shone high and bright all day long.

"On that Sunday, I looked out through the window – it must have been about 10 o'clock in the morning – and to be honest I was a bit scared," says John. "The amount of people, physically... I thought, 'where are they all going to go?'"

"But when we watched it on television after, we got a real buzz," he says. "It showed the spectators going up the field, and we thought 'We helped make that happen.' It was unbelievable – we'll never see anything like that again round here!"

Perhaps more than anything else in the village's history, the 2014 Tour de France put Bradfield on the map. And Bradfield Brewery was right at the centre of it all.

82

At the heart of the
COMMUNITY

Watt House Farm was always an integral part of Bradfield, serving the village with milk for decades. When it became the home of Bradfield Brewery as well, the Gills were keen for that trend to continue.

"I think it's important to be involved with the community," says John Gill. "It's all about giving something back."

Being firm fans of sport, the Gills have always been keen to support their local clubs. The brewery sponsor Bradfield Cricket Club, Stocksbridge Rugby Club and Oughtibridge Football Club, and in the past have also sponsored the Sheffield Tigers speedway team, based at nearby Owlerton Stadium.

"The football team have the brewery logo on their hoodies – so if you go into Oughtibridge on a Saturday, it's Bradfield Brewery across the board!" laughs Pete Jackson. "The family are really good with their sponsorships and being part of the community."

But above all others, one sport has played an enormous part in the Gills' lives – and as John explains, it's perhaps not the pastime one would expect this farming family to be into...

"My mate used to own a garage at Low Bradfield, and one day in 1994 he told me he'd got an invitation to one of the suites at the Sheffield Arena to watch the ice hockey, through his motor trade connections," says John. "I told him I wasn't interested."

"Reluctantly I went with him," John says, "And right from when the game first started, with the music blaring and kids dancing, players fighting on the ice and scoring goals, it just gave me a buzz."

"I came back home and said 'Right, next weekend we're going down as a family,'" he says. "Since then, me and Susan have hardly ever missed a game."

John, Susan and their children became stalwart supporters of the team, the Sheffield Steelers, following them across the country and even overseas. Years later, when they made the move into brewing, they were approached by an ex-player, Mike O'Connor. Now working as the Steelers' commercial manager, Mike asked if Bradfield Brewery were interested in sponsoring the team.

Needless to say they were. At first, the brewery sponsored an individual player – which meant that whenever that player scored, their name was read out over the arena's booming speaker system. Season by season, Bradfield Brewery continued their sponsorship, and in 2011 decided to step up their involvement and have their name emblazoned on the team's jerseys.

"We'd agreed a deal and put some money up front," says John. "Then one morning, we were sat having breakfast, and it came on the local news that the Steelers had gone bust!"

Fortunately, the team recovered, and the new owner kindly honoured the deal Bradfield Brewery had made. The Gills are still fans and sponsors of the Steelers to this day – but this episode led the family to look elsewhere for an extra fix of their favourite sport.

Through a business connection, the family were introduced to Andre Payette, who had played professional hockey in his homeland of Canada. He had moved to England to take over as head coach of the Sheffield Steeldogs, a team in the league below the Steelers.

"We got on with him well, so we went down to a couple of games and liked what we saw," says John. "We became title sponsors the following year, and we've carried on ever since."

Their status as title sponsors means the team's official name is now the Bradfield Brewery Sheffield Steeldogs – a fact which still makes John and the family proud every time they see it on jerseys and billboards.

In over a decade of brewing, the Gills have had their fair share of proud moments. For Lisa, one occasion sticks in the mind which harks back to the family's farming roots:

"One thing I'll always remember is when our horses were chosen to lead the Stannington Gala," says Lisa of the annual event in Bradfield's neighbouring village. "I was taking pictures of it, and it just got me – the fact that our horses were in front. That was a special moment."

Of course, Bradfield Brewery is an extended family, with staff who have been with the Gills from the very beginning. Together, they have built the brewery – literally – into what it is today.

"I've seen all the family grow up, especially Richard and Lisa – they've got kids of their own now," says head brewer Paul Ward. "When I came here, it was like a dusty lane, and looking at it now you can see how it's progressed. Setting up the brewery was a risk, but you've got to take risks to succeed sometimes, and it's paid off for us all."

"I can't believe it's got so big so quickly," says Pete Jackson. "Ten years might sound like a long time, but it isn't in business. I also think it happened at just the right moment, with real ale coming back into fashion again. Some beers are better than others, but all ours are fairly easy drinking – they speak for themselves. Although obviously we're biased!"

Watt House Farm was something John and Susan had built up, once they had taken it over from Susan's family. But, says John, the credit for Bradfield Brewery's success should go instead to the next generation...

"People often say to me 'How did you have the guts to go into brewing?'" he says. "I think if it was just me and Susan, we wouldn't have done – we'd have carried on doing what we were doing and tried to make farming pay. The reason we had the confidence to set up the brewery was that we had Richard, and Lisa behind us, to bounce off."

"We gave them the opportunity to learn – I think you've got to hand it forward," John continues. "At least I know now, if I went off this mortal earth tomorrow, the brewery would go on, and go on well. That means we've done a good job as parents."

Like Pete, John is amazed at how far things have progressed in a relatively short amount of time.

"It's not until people say to you 'Look what you've done' that you do actually sit back and take stock," he says. "I still take things on a day-to-day basis. But it has come a long way, from me and Susan going up to Newcastle with six casks of beer in the back of a van, to all this..."

"I think what I'm particularly most proud of is that since we started, we've ploughed money back into the farm," John says. "We've smartened all the buildings up. But hopefully it still looks like a farm – we've tried not to alter the feel of it."

"That's been our philosophy from the very beginning," says John. "Put things back in and make it a bit better. It sees us well."

And it sees the rest of us well too. Thanks to that investment, that willingness to go out on a limb, this farming family swapped pints of milk for pints of beer – and legions of fans up and down the country are glad they did. Raise a glass, then, to Bradfield Brewery – serving up a true taste of tradition.

A question of
TASTE

Matching beer with food? Surely not! As any self-respecting gourmand knows, the only proper accompaniment to a good meal is fine wine. Isn't that right?

Not necessarily. As brewing techniques have improved, the beers being produced have grown more varied in terms of flavour and taste. Today's beers are a perfect partner to cuisines of all kinds – every bit as sophisticated as the very best wines.

Bradfield Brewery's beers are, of course, delicious enjoyed on their own. But they make an ideal match for a wide range of meals as well. From savoury snacks to hearty dinners, they all taste even better washed down with a glass of Farmers.

When the idea came to produce a book about the Bradfield Brewery story, the Gill family knew they also wanted to include some mouth-watering recipes – dishes that work beautifully alongside their beers, and even some which use Bradfield ale as an ingredient. Being lovers of fish 'n' chips and the flavours of the sea, the Gills wanted the focus to be on seafood. And for help in coming up with some suitably impressive fish dishes, they turned to the best in the business: their good friends at the Magpie Café.

From a distinctive black and white building overlooking Whitby harbour, the Magpie Café has been serving fabulous fish, chips and seafood since 1939. Ian and Alison Robinson took over from Alison's parents in 1990, and since then, with the help of head chef Paul Gildroy, they have made the Magpie the best 'chippy' in the country. Listed in all major food guides and acclaimed by leading critics and the public alike, the Magpie has become a true Yorkshire landmark.

Bradfield Brewery have supplied the Magpie's café-restaurant with beer for many years, so Ian and Paul were only too happy to share some of their recipes in return. First, though, it would have to be decided which dishes would marry best with which of Bradfield's beers. So on a crisp and sunny day, John and Richard met with Ian and Paul at the Magpie to talk – and taste – it over...

Farmers Blonde

(ABV 4.0%)

John: This was one of the first two 'specials' we did after we'd brewed our first three 'core' beers, which were Farmers Bitter, later rebranded Farmers Ale; Farmers Pale Ale; and Farmers Stout. After that, our first specials were Farmers Brown Cow and Farmers Blonde, both named after breeds of cow: Swiss Brown, and a French breed call Blonde d'Aquitaine.

The Blonde turned out to be really popular; it's always been our best seller. As you can see it's a real pale colour. The reason for that is that we wanted to get a beer as light as we could. When in a bottle it's carbonated, so it's as near to a lager as we get.

Richard: It's a good session beer, this – our best by a long way.

Paul: Both the nose and the taste are just spot on. It's citrusy, which would cut through the richness of fish 'n' chips very well.

"The Blonde turned out to be really popular; it's always been our best-seller."

Yorkshire Farmer

(ABV 4.0%)

Richard: This one is a bit more of a bitter, another session beer.

John: Yorkshire Farmer has been in production for about seven years. We keep doing specials all the time, and when they are really popular, they become a regular. This is one of those.

It's more of a traditional bitter colour than the Blonde. People around Sheffield liken it to the colour of the old Stones Bitter. It is similar, but a bit more characteristic, we like to think.

Paul: I can't drink many bitters, but this is a lovely one; a very smooth finish. It reminds me of Newcastle Brown Ale.

Ian: There's a spiciness to it as well, so it would go well with spicy food – maybe a fish curry.

"This is a lovely one.
A very smooth finish."

Farmers Pale Ale

(ABV 5.0%)

John: This is my particular favourite. It's the one I usually sample when I go down to our pub, to make sure it's travelled alright from the brewery! Again, it's very pale, but it's got a bit more body to it than the Blonde.

Richard: It's just got that bit more sweetness, which carries through in a bottle.

When you bottle beer, you're filtering it as well. It's then re-carbonated, so it is played about with a bit. It does alter the taste slightly, but there's nothing else you can do to give it a good shelf-life. We have done bottle-conditioned beer before, which is where you have yeast in the bottle which settles down on the bottom, so it's still a living product. But you can't get the right consistency with it.

Paul: This would go well with a tomato-based pasta – a vongole or something like that, with clams. It's got a citrusy finish to it, so that would work well with a light seafood pasta. With the Blonde, you get that citrus kick at the beginning, whereas with this one it follows through.

"This is my particular favourite. It's the one I usually sample when I go down to our pub, to make sure it's travelled alright from the brewery!"

Farmers Brown Cow

(ABV 4.2%)

John: Straight away you can see that this is considerably darker. For our first two specials, we wanted a complete contrast, one light and one dark.

Richard: You can smell the difference in this one as well – it's a lot more malty.

Ian: This one would be my favourite.

Paul: I would say with this, because it has a nice dry finish to it, it would certainly go with a buttery or creamy sauce – it would cut through. There are endless options. Most of the dishes on our menu have butter or cream in them! Another option is oysters, which always go well with beer – steak and ale pie with oysters, for example.

"Because it has a nice dry finish to it, it would certainly go with a buttery or creamy sauce. Most of the dishes on our menu have butter or cream in them!"

Farmers Sixer

(ABV 6.0%)

John: We were approached by Simon Moreman at Sixer Magazine, which distributes to the Sheffield 6 postcode area which the brewery is in, to brew a beer. The obvious thing to do was to make a 6 per cent beer.

The first time we ever brewed it, we had a bit of a sampling session in the brewery. All the lads were sat round, and we had about three pints each. We were saying "It's not strong, this – it doesn't taste like 6 per cent." And then we tried to get off our stools! It's a very deceiving stronger beer – usually stronger beer has more of a taste to it. I think what disguises the strength is the sweetness.

Paul: You're right. If you didn't know you wouldn't be able to tell that this is such a strong beer. I can feel it warming me up!

Ian: Food-wise, this would work well with something meaty like a halibut, or a savoury dish like a ratatouille.

"If you didn't know you wouldn't be able to tell that this is such a strong beer. I can feel it warming me up!"

Farmers Stout

(ABV 4.5%)

John: This is another one of our original three. We've often thought about what we did wrong: coming from a dairy farming background, we ought to have called it 'Milk Stout'!

Paul: It's very chocolatey on the nose, isn't it?

John: This is one that I do like carbonated.

Richard: I prefer it on draught. It's a lot smoother.

John: I think you often get people that say: "Oh, I don't like stout." I think it's because they're not used to that sort of flavour. But when they actually try it, they say: "It's not bad!" When people ask me what Farmers Stout is like, I say it's halfway between a Guinness and a Mackeson. Guinness is a bit harsh-tasting, Mackeson is really sweet, and I think ours is somewhere in the middle.

Richard: There's a roasted barley, coffee sort of taste. A 'burnt' flavour.

John: It's the same type of barley in all our beers, just toasted to different levels – some are roasted, some slightly roasted. That's the only difference between a light beer and a dark one: it isn't a different product going into the beer, it's just more toasted.

Richard: This stout only has a small amount of roasted barley – 1 per cent.

John: It takes very little to turn it from light to dark.

Paul: This will take on a lot of flavours.

Richard: I'd have it with a fish pie.

Paul: Yeah, a creamy sauce – it would complement it. There are bold flavours in there – I can taste tarragon.

RECIPES

Baked halibut with pea and ham

Serves 4

Ingredients

4 x 200g fillets of halibut
1 ham hock
400g dried marrowfat peas
1 teaspoon bicarbonate of soda
50g butter
1 medium onion, roughly chopped
2 cloves crushed garlic
1 teaspoon sugar
Pea green colouring (optional)
400-450ml ham stock (the cooking liquor from the hock)
Oil, for cooking
Salt and pepper, to season
Cress, to garnish (optional)

Method

For the ham hock
Place the ham into a pan and completely cover with water.

Bring to the boil and reduce to a gentle simmer. Cook for around 2 and a half to 3 hours, or until the meat will pull away from the bone. Remove the hock, cool it enough to handle and strip all the meat off the bone. Pass the cooking liquor (ham stock) through a sieve and set aside (400-450ml).

For the peas
Wash the peas in cold water at least twice. Cover them with three times as much water, stir in the bicarbonate of soda and leave to soak overnight.

The next day, rinse the peas twice again. In a deep pan, melt the butter and add the onion and garlic. After a couple of minutes add the peas, sugar, colouring (if using) and ham stock. The peas should be covered with liquid; top up with water if necessary.

Bring to the boil and cook for around 45 minutes, or until the peas are soft and losing their shape. Taste, and add salt and pepper if needed.

For the halibut
Pre-heat the oven to 220°C / Gas Mark 8.

Heat a little oil in a pan and carefully lay in each piece of fish, flesh side down. Cook for 3 to 4 minutes then turn the fish over. Add to the pan the stripped ham hock pieces, then place the pan into the pre-heated oven for 6 minutes.

To serve
Scatter the ham hock pieces over the mushy peas and sit the halibut on top. Garnish with cress if desired.

Rump, Farmers Stout and oyster pie

Serves 6

Ingredients

750g diced rump steak
500ml Farmers Stout
6 shucked oysters
150g plain flour
2 carrots, finely diced
2 large onions, finely diced
1 fennel bulb, finely diced
2 bulbs crushed garlic
2 tablespoons tomato purée
2 teaspoons English mustard
500ml beef stock
Oil, for cooking
Salt and pepper, to season

For the pastry
350g self-raising flour
175g beef suet
Ice cold water, to bind
Milk or beaten egg, to coat
Salt and pepper, to season

Method

Place the rump in a bowl with the stout, cover and place in the fridge overnight to marinate.
The next day, strain the meat, reserving the marinade. Place the meat into a bowl and dust with 100g of the flour, salt and pepper.
Heat a little oil in a pan and in small batches brown the meat. Once all the meat has been browned, set it aside, then add to the pan the carrot, onion, fennel and garlic. Sauté until golden, then add the remaining 50g of flour and mix in well.
Add the tomato purée and mustard, stir in and then return the meat to the pan.
Cook for a couple of minutes before adding the stout marinade. This will thicken the mixture; stir well. Add the beef stock and stir. Bring to the boil then reduce to a simmer. Cook gently for 1 and a half to 2 hours or until the meat is tender. Remove the meat from the heat and allow to cool.

For the pastry
Sieve the flour into a bowl with some salt and pepper. Add the suet and mix through using a fork. Pour in ice cold water, enough to bind the ingredients together and form a smooth dough. Wrap this with clingfilm and rest in the fridge for a minimum of 1 hour.

To cook
Pre-heat the oven to 185°C / Gas Mark 6.
Once the pastry is chilled, remove it from the fridge and divide into 6 equal pieces. Take 6 pie tins or bowls and share the meat between them. Sit a shucked oyster on top of the meat.
Roll out each piece of pastry to a size big enough to cover each dish (the pastry needs to be quite thick, around a centimetre). Cover the dishes with the pastry and trim the edges. Prick a couple of holes into the top and brush the pastry with either milk or egg wash.
Place the pies into the pre-heated oven for around 35 to 40 minutes, or until the pastry is golden and you see gravy bubbling out of the sides.
Serve immediately with thick cut chips and mushy peas.

Seared local scallops, black pudding, pease pudding and spiced tomato sauce

Serves 2

Ingredients

6 king scallops
150g black pudding, cut into cubes
Oil, for cooking
Fresh herbs, to garnish (optional)

For the pease pudding
500g yellow split peas
4 rashers smoked streaky bacon
Half medium onion
1 medium potato
100g butter
2 egg yolks
Salt and pepper, to season

For the sauce
1 x 400g tin chopped tomatoes
Half carrot, finely diced
2 shallots, finely diced
Quarter stick celery, finely diced
1 chilli, finely diced
1 clove crushed garlic
Half teaspoon chopped parsley
Oil, for cooking
Salt and pepper, to season

Method

For the pease pudding
Soak the yellow split peas overnight. The next day, wash them again and drain. Pre-heat the oven to 160°C / Gas Mark 4.
Roughly chop the bacon, onion and potato and place into a pan with the split peas. Cover with water, bring to the boil and simmer for around 1 hour or until the peas are tender.
Drain off any excess water and place the mix into a food processor. Blitz until smooth and add the butter and egg yolks. Season with salt and pepper, then pour the mix into an ovenproof dish. Put this into the pre-heated oven for around 40 minutes or until it feels firm to the touch.
Chill the pease pudding down then cut it into small cubes. This would be best done the day before to give time to set up properly.

For the sauce
Heat a little oil in a pan and add the diced carrot, shallot, celery, chilli and garlic. Sauté gently for a couple of minutes, without any colour. Add the tomatoes and bring to the boil, then reduce the heat and simmer for about 30 minutes. Season to taste and add the chopped parsley. Set aside and keep warm.

To cook
Heat a little oil in a pan and lay in the scallops clockwise around the pan. Add the black pudding and pease pudding into the spaces around the scallops and sauté for 1 and a half minutes. Turn the scallops over, then likewise the black pudding and pease pudding, and cook for a further 1 and a half minutes.

To serve
Spoon some of the tomato sauce onto plates then arrange the scallops, black pudding and pease pudding on top of and around the sauce. Finish with some fresh herbs if desired.

Bread brill fillet with Spanish potatoes

Serves 4

Ingredients

4 x 200g fillets of brill
100g plain flour
3 eggs, beaten
150g white breadcrumbs
100g capers
50g butter
1 tablespoon chopped parsley
Oil, for cooking
Salt and pepper, to season
Lemon wedges, to serve

For the Spanish potatoes

400g baby potatoes
2 tablespoons oil
1 large onion, finely sliced
2 red chillies, finely chopped
3-4 cloves crushed garlic
2 x 400g tins chopped tomatoes
Salt and pepper, to season

Method

For the Spanish potatoes

Pre-heat the oven to 210°C / Gas Mark 7.

Add the oil to a roasting tray and heat in the pre-heated oven. Add the potatoes and cook until lightly brown. Add the sliced onion, chillies and garlic and cook for a further couple of minutes. Add the chopped tomatoes, some salt and pepper to season and stir well. Cover with a lid or foil, then place into the pre-heated oven for about 20-25 minutes, or until the potatoes are tender and the sauce has reduced slightly.

For the brill

Place the flour into a bowl and season with salt and pepper. Place the beaten egg into another bowl and the breadcrumbs into a third bowl. Take one of the brill fillets, lay it into the flour, shake off any excess, then coat with the beaten egg, then the breadcrumbs.

Pre-heat a pan with a little oil and lay in the fillet of brill, flesh side down. Cook for about 4 minutes, then turn the fish over and cook for a further 4 minutes.

Remove from the pan and place onto kitchen paper to drain. Place in the lower part of the oven to keep warm, then prepare the other fillets in the same way – coating with the flour, egg and breadcrumbs, then cooking in the pan. Do one at a time.

Once all the fish are cooked, add the capers, butter and parsley to the same pan. Cook for a couple of minutes to make a sauce.

To serve

Place a spoonful of Spanish potatoes onto your plate, lay the brill fillet on top and then pour the caper, butter and parsley sauce over the top. Serve with the lemon wedges.

Coley with mussel and potato chowder

Serves 4

Ingredients

4 x 200g skinless coley fillets
8 slices prosciutto ham
Oil, for cooking
Salt and pepper, to season

For the chowder
500g mussels
4 shallots, sliced
1 clove crushed garlic
4 medium potatoes, diced
1 bay leaf
200ml fish stock
200ml milk
200ml double cream
25g soft butter and 25g flour mixed
together into a paste (beurre manie)
1 handful chopped parsley
Oil, for cooking
Salt and pepper, to season

For the pesto
100g sun blush tomatoes
50g pine kernels
1 clove garlic
1 handful basil
150ml olive oil

Method

For the pesto
Simply blitz together all the ingredients and set aside for later.

For the chowder
Heat a little oil in a pan, add the shallots and garlic and sauté until softened. Add the potatoes, bay leaf and stock, bring to the boil and cook for 12 minutes.

Add the mussels, cover with a lid or foil and cook for a further 4 to 5 minutes, or until the mussels have opened and potatoes are tender. Remove the potatoes, mussels and bay leaf from the pan and set aside.

Once cool enough to handle, remove around half the mussels from their shells and return this mussel meat to the potatoes and remaining mussels.

Add the milk and cream to the pan of stock and bring to the boil. Whisk in the beurre manie and bring back to the boil. This will thicken the sauce slightly, but if it is too thick just add a little more cream.

Return the mussels, mussel meat and potatoes to the pan, add salt and pepper to taste and finish with the chopped parsley.

For the coley
Wrap the coley with the prosciutto (two slices per fillet), heat a little oil in a pan and lay in the fish. Over a high heat, seal the fish all round, then place the pan into a hot oven for 6 minutes.

Lift the pan out of the oven, pour the pesto over the fish and return to the oven for a further 3 minutes.

To serve
Divide the chowder between 4 bowls and sit the coley on top.

Crab crusted halibut with beetroot Dauphinoise

Serves 4

Ingredients

4 x 200g halibut fillets
50g butter
3 slices stale white bread
50g brown crab meat, chopped up
80g white crab meat, chopped up
1 tablespoon parsley
Squeeze of lemon juice
300g kale
Oil, for cooking
Salt and pepper, to season

For the beetroot dauphinoise
1kg fresh beetroot
400ml milk
200ml double cream
2 cloves crushed garlic
1 tablespoon horseradish sauce
Salt and pepper, to season

Method

For the beetroot dauphinoise
Pre-heat the oven to 180°C / Gas Mark 6.

Peel and very thinly slice the beetroot, and layer into an ovenproof dish.

Heat the milk, cream, garlic and horseradish together in a pan over a low heat for 10 minutes to infuse, season with salt and pepper and pour over the beetroot. Cover the dish with foil and place into the pre-heated oven for 1 hour. Remove the foil and bake for a further 18 minutes. Set aside ready to be reheated later.

For the halibut
Turn the oven up to 220°C / Gas Mark 8.
Blitz the bread to a fine crumb. Melt the butter in a pan and add the crumb. Over a medium heat, lightly toast the crumb, stirring constantly. Remove the pan from the heat.

Combine both brown and white crab meats together, add the parsley and lemon juice, then stir into the breadcrumbs.

Place the halibut onto an ovenproof tray, season with salt and pepper then top with the crumb. Bake in the oven for 8 minutes, or until the crumb is a rich golden brown.

Meanwhile, sauté the kale in a pan with a little oil over a medium to high heat until wilted, and season well. Place the dauphinoise back in the oven for a couple of minutes until heated through.

To serve
Place a good spoonful of beetroot dauphinoise onto your plate. Next to that sit some kale, top with the baked halibut and serve immediately.

Haddock with 'Yorkshire Blue' cauliflower cheese

Serves 2

Ingredients

2 x 200g haddock fillets
2 slices white bread
Half a leek, finely sliced
200g Yorkshire Blue cheese
50g butter
2 shallots, finely sliced
50g plain flour
300ml full fat milk
1 small cauliflower
Handful mixed salad leaves
Dressing (2 tablespoons lemon juice,
4 tablespoons olive oil, pepper to
taste)
Oil, for cooking
Salt and pepper, to season

Method

Blitz the slices of bread in a food processor until fine.

Heat a little oil in a pan over a medium heat and add the sliced leek. Sauté for a couple of minutes until softened then add the breadcrumbs. Cook until the breadcrumbs have turned golden in colour.

Remove from the heat and crumble in 50g of the Yorkshire Blue cheese. Set aside.

Season the haddock with salt and pepper. In a clean pan, heat a little oil and carefully lay in the fish. Pan-fry for 3 to 4 minutes, then turn the fish over and cook for a further 3 to 4 minutes.

In another clean pan, melt the butter and add the shallots. Sauté for a minute, then add the flour. Cook for a couple of minutes until the flour takes on a sandy texture. Gradually add the milk, a little at a time, stirring continuously until all the milk has been added.

Bring the sauce to the boil, reduce the heat and simmer for a couple of minutes. The sauce consistency should be that of thick double cream; it should coat the back of a spoon. Whisk in the remaining Yorkshire Blue, taste and season if necessary.

Finally, bring a pan of salted water to boil. Cut the cauliflower into florets and plunge into the water for 3 to 4 minutes or until tender. Strain the cauliflower and divide onto 2 plates. Pour over the cheese sauce and top with the breadcrumbs, then place the haddock beside the cauliflower. Lightly dress the salad leaves and place some on top of the haddock to garnish.

Hake goujons with BBQ dip

Serves 4

Ingredients

400g hake fillet, cut into strips
approximately 10cm long
100g plain flour
3 eggs, beaten
150g white breadcrumbs
Oil, for cooking
Salt and pepper, to season

For the sauce
800g tin chopped tomatoes
1 medium onion, chopped
2 sticks celery, chopped
1 clove garlic
Half teaspoon ground ginger
1 teaspoon smoked paprika
Half teaspoon Chinese five spice
2 tablespoons tomato ketchup
1 tablespoon Worcestershire sauce
75ml white wine vinegar
60g dark brown sugar
Oil, for cooking
Salt and pepper, to season

Method

For the sauce
In a pan, heat a little oil and add the onion, celery and garlic. Cook for 3 to 4 minutes until lightly coloured, then add the tomatoes, spices, ketchup and Worcestershire sauce. Bring to the boil and reduce to a simmer.

In a separate pan, boil together the vinegar and sugar to a light syrup. Add this to the tomatoes and cook for around 25 to 30 minutes or until thickened slightly. Blitz in a food processor until smooth and season to taste.

For the hake
Place the flour into a bowl and season with salt and pepper. Place the beaten egg into another bowl and the breadcrumbs into a third bowl. Take one of the hake strips, lay it into the flour, shake off any excess, then coat with the beaten egg, then the breadcrumbs. Repeat this process with each piece of fish to double coat.

Deep-fry the hake goujons until golden and crispy; they should take about 4 to 6 minutes to cook. Drain the goujons on kitchen paper to remove any excess oil and season with a little salt.

To serve
Place the goujons in a serving basket. Serve the warm BBQ sauce in a separate bowl for dipping.

Kipper kedgeree

Serves 2

Ingredients

2 kippers
200g basmati rice
1 tablespoon oil
1 small onion, finely chopped
1 teaspoon curry paste
150ml milk
100ml double cream
2 hardboiled eggs
1 knob butter
1 tablespoon chopped coriander
Salt and pepper, to season
Lemon wedges, to serve

Method

Cook the kippers by poaching them in water for 3 to 4 minutes, remove them from the pan and set aside. Once cooled enough to handle, pick the meat from the kippers and put to one side.

For the rice, heat the tablespoon of oil in a pan and add the onion. Sauté for a minute, then add the curry paste and cook for a further minute.

Add the rice and stir in the milk and cream. Bring to the boil and reduce to a very gentle simmer. Place a lid on the pan and cook for around 10 to 12 minutes, or until the liquid has been absorbed and the rice is cooked. Add a little water if the rice becomes too dry.

Chop the boiled eggs into quarters or eighths and stir through the rice, together with the butter, coriander, pepper and meat from the kipper. Check the seasoning and serve immediately with wedges of lemon.

Lobster carbonara

Serves 2

Ingredients

1 whole cooked dressed lobster
100g dried pasta (spaghetti or
tagliatelle)
100g smoked pancetta
2 banana shallots, thinly sliced
1 clove crushed garlic
250ml double cream
30g butter
1 egg yolk
30g Parmesan cheese, grated
1 tablespoon chopped parsley
Oil, for cooking
Salt and pepper, to season
Ciabatta, to serve (optional)

Method

Place the pasta into boiling salted water and cook as per packet instructions.

Meanwhile, cut the pancetta into small lardons and place into a pan with a tiny amount of oil. Cook until golden in colour, then add the sliced shallots and crushed garlic. Sauté for a couple of minutes then add the cream. Bring to the boil and then reduce to a simmer. Whilst the cream is coming to the boil, cut up the meat of the lobster. Once the cream is simmering, add the lobster to warm through.

Add the butter and swirl the pan to mix in. Remove the pan from the heat and whisk in the egg yolk, then the grated Parmesan. Strain the pasta and add it to the lobster cream, together with the chopped parsley and salt and pepper to taste. Toss the pasta thoroughly through the cream and share between two plates. Serve immediately with fresh ciabatta if desired.

Monkfish and sausage casserole

Serves 2

Ingredients

400g monkfish fillet, cut into 6
pieces
150ml red wine
200g pork mince
2 slices smoked streaky bacon,
finely chopped
1 slice white bread, blitzed to a fine
crumb
5g fresh sage, chopped
1 teaspoon dried marjoram
1 teaspoon chopped parsley
Splash of port
100ml chicken stock
1 small carrot, finely chopped
Half a leek, finely chopped
1 x 400g tin chopped tomatoes
Oil, for cooking
Salt and pepper, to season

Method

Place the monkfish in a pan and marinade in the red wine for a minimum of 2 hours before cooking.

To make the sausage, mix together the pork mince, bacon, breadcrumbs, herbs, port, salt and pepper. Split the mixture into 16 and roll into balls. You will only need half of these so chill or freeze the rest for another time.

Heat a little oil in a pan over a moderate heat and add the sausage balls, browning them all around. Pour about half of the red wine that the monkfish has been marinating in into the pan and reduce by two-thirds. Add the stock, carrot and leek, cook for a minute and then add the tomatoes. Bring to the boil and then reduce to a simmer. Add the monkfish, cover the pan with a lid and cook for 6 to 8 minutes until the monkfish is cooked. Taste the sauce and adjust the seasoning to your taste. Serve with plenty of herby mashed potatoes.

Mussels with Farmers Blonde and pancetta

Serves 4

Ingredients

2kg fresh mussels
300ml Farmers Blonde
100g pancetta, cut into lardons
75g butter
6 shallots, finely sliced
1 clove crushed garlic
6 spring onions, roughly chopped
100g halved cherry tomatoes
150ml double cream
1 tablespoon chopped parsley
Ciabatta, to serve

Method

Melt the butter in a deep pan, and sauté the pancetta until cooked and golden. Add the shallots and garlic and cook until soft and translucent.

Wash the mussels and remove any beards (if any are open, tap them and they should close; if they don't, throw them away). Add the mussels to the pan with the Farmers Blonde and cover with a tight-fitting lid. Cook for about 4 to 5 minutes, shaking the pan occasionally.

Lift off the lid and check that the mussels have opened; if they have not opened, cook for a little longer. Discard any that do not open – do not eat them.

Add the spring onions, tomatoes and cream, bring back to the boil and reduce the liquor by a quarter.

To serve
Divide the mussels evenly between 4 bowls, then add the chopped parsley to the liquor. Share the liquor between the bowls and serve with loads of fresh ciabatta to mop up the sauce.

Pakora skate cheeks

Serves 4-6

Ingredients

400g skate or cod cheeks
Juice of 2 limes
2 teaspoons garam masala
1 tablespoon fresh coriander, finely
chopped
Sunflower or vegetable oil, for deep
frying
Salt and pepper, to season

For the batter
200g gram flour (chickpea flour)
2 teaspoons ground turmeric
1 teaspoon cayenne pepper
1 red chilli, very finely chopped
2 shallots, very finely chopped
200ml ice cold water
Salt and pepper, to season

Method

In a bowl, mix together the lime juice, garam masala and coriander. Season well with salt and pepper then add the pieces of fish. Toss the cheeks in the marinade, cover the bowl with clingfilm and place into the fridge for about an hour, turning the fish occasionally.

For the batter
In a bowl, place the gram flour, turmeric, cayenne pepper, chilli and shallot. Season with salt and pepper, then gradually whisk in the chilled water until the batter resembles double cream (you may need a little less or a little more water). Cover the bowl with clingfilm and place into the fridge to rest.

To cook
Heat the oil in a pan to around 175ºC (the oil should not be more than halfway up the pan). Once it has heated up, take the fish and batter from the fridge. Dip each piece of fish into the batter and then carefully into the hot oil. Deep fry for 6 to 7 minutes or until the batter is golden and crisp (this is best done in small batches). Drain on kitchen paper and serve immediately with a selection of dips such as minted yoghurt or mango chutney.

Pan fried skate wing with warm pickle salad

Serves 2

Ingredients

2 x 350g skate wings
200g new potatoes
Plain flour, for dusting
6 gherkins
2 pickled onions
2 spring onions
Sprig of fresh tarragon
1 tablespoon capers
Olive oil, to dress
Oil, for cooking
Salt and pepper, to season

Method

Place the potatoes into boiling salted water and cook until tender. Drain and keep warm.

Season some plain flour with salt and pepper, then dust the skate wings with the flour, knocking off any excess. Heat a little oil in a frying pan and carefully lay in the fish, thickest side first. Pan fry for around 4 minutes or until golden in colour, then turn the fish over and cook for a further 4 to 5 minutes. Once cooked, remove from the pan and sit on kitchen paper.

Whilst the skate is cooking, thinly slice the gherkins, pickled onions and spring onions. Add these to the cooked potatoes and drizzle over a little olive oil. Season with salt and pepper and toss till well mixed. Tear the tarragon leaves, add to the potatoes along with the capers and toss to mix.

To serve
Place the skate wing onto the plate and spoon on a generous portion of the potatoes. Serve immediately with fresh mayonnaise.

Pan fried turbot with ratatouille

Serves 4

Ingredients

4 x 200g fillets of turbot
2 courgettes
1 large aubergine
1 large onion
1 red pepper
1 yellow pepper
100g fine beans
1 head broccoli
500g ripe tomatoes
2 cloves crushed garlic
2 tablespoons chopped parsley
Oil, for cooking
Salt and pepper, to season
Basil leaves, to garnish (optional)

Method

Cut the courgettes into slices and lay them onto a baking tray. Lightly cover with salt, then clingfilm and leave for about an hour to draw out some of the bitterness.

Roughly chop the aubergine and onion and slice the peppers. Cut the fine beans in half and the broccoli into florets. Cut the tomatoes into quarters, lightly squeeze to remove the majority of the seeds then roughly chop the flesh.

Heat a little oil in a pan and add the onion, peppers and crushed garlic. Sauté for a couple of minutes then add the chopped tomatoes. Cook for about 15 minutes or until some of the liquid has evaporated. Rinse the courgettes and add them to the tomato along with the aubergines. Cook for 5 minutes, add the fine beans and broccoli and cook for a further 3 to 4 minutes. Season with salt and pepper and stir through the chopped parsley. Set aside whilst you pan fry the turbot.

Heat a little oil in a pan, season the fish with salt and pepper and gently lay in each piece of fish, flesh side down. Pan fry for about 4 minutes, then turn the fish over and cook for a further 4 minutes.

To serve
Spoon some of the ratatouille onto the plate and lay on the turbot so that it slightly overlaps. Serve with baby roast potatoes and garnish with basil leaves if desired.

Salmon salsa burger

Serves 4

Ingredients

For the burgers
600g fresh skinless salmon
3 spring onions, finely chopped
20g fresh breadcrumbs
1 tablespoon chopped chives
1 clove crushed garlic
3 tablespoons mayonnaise
Pinch of smoked paprika
Salt and pepper, to season

For the salsa
5 tomatoes, skinned, deseeded and
finely diced
1 medium red onion, finely diced
1-2 red chillies, seeds removed and
finely diced
Juice of 1 lime (you could also add a
little zest to give a more intense
burst of lime flavour)
1 teaspoon caster sugar
3-4 tablespoons chopped coriander

Oil, for cooking
4 soft flour bread baps (or bread of
your choice)
Little gem lettuce leaves, to serve
Soured cream, to serve
Jalapeño chillies, to serve (optional)

Method

For the salsa
Mix all ingredients together and taste – you may need to add more chilli or lime. Cover and chill. Make this in advance so the flavours develop.

For the burger
Place the salmon into a food processor and blitz until almost smooth. Add all the rest of the ingredients and blitz until well mixed. Remove the mix from the bowl and divide into 4 equal amounts. Mould into wheel shapes, around 2cm thick. Place into a fridge to rest for a minimum of 30 minutes before cooking.

To cook
Pre-heat a pan and add a little oil. Gently lay in the salmon burgers and cook over a moderate heat for about 3 minutes. Turn the burgers over and cook for a further 3 minutes. The burgers will feel bouncy when they are cooked, but if you are unsure just pierce the centre with the tip of a knife and gently open to see if they are cooked through. If not, simply cook a little longer.

To serve
Slice the bread baps in half and toast. Sit some little gem lettuce onto the bottom half of the bread bap and place the burger on top, then a good spoon of salsa followed by some soured cream. If you want a little extra kick, add slices of jalapeño chillies. Finish with the top half of bread bap. Serve with sweet potato wedges.

Scampi wrap with pea guacamole

Serves 4

Ingredients

1 250g bag wholetail Whitby
Seafoods scampi
4 flour tortilla wraps
1-2 little gem lettuce/s
Sweet potato fries, to serve

For the pea guacamole
200g garden peas
30g sugar
Squeeze of lime
2 pickled onions, roughly chopped
2 tablespoon mayonnaise
3 gherkins, finely chopped
1 tablespoon capers, finely chopped
1 red chilli, finely chopped
1 teaspoon wholegrain mustard
1 tablespoon chopped parsley

Method

For the pea guacamole
Cook the garden peas as instructed on the packet. Drain and place into a food processor with the sugar, squeeze of lime and pickled onions. Blitz until smooth, then add the mayonnaise and mix well. Remove the pea guacamole from the food processor and fold in the gherkins, capers, chilli, mustard and parsley. Cover and place into the fridge to chill.

For the scampi
Cook the scampi and sweet potato fries as instructed on the packets. Once cooked place them onto kitchen paper to drain.

Warm the tortilla and spread the pea guacamole over about two-thirds of the wrap. Sit the scampi on top with a few leaves of lettuce and roll up the tortilla. Serve with the sweet potato fries.

Seafood jambalaya

Serves 4

Ingredients

16 king prawn tails, peeled and deveined
100g salmon
20 mussels, cleaned and beards removed
160g prepared squid, cleaned and scored
100g smoked salmon, cut into strips
1 red onion, thinly sliced
1 sliced red pepper
1 sliced green pepper
2 rashers unsmoked streaky bacon
100g chorizo, cut into small dice
2 chillies, finely chopped (leave the seeds in if you prefer the dish to be hot)
2 cloves crushed garlic
2 teaspoons Cajun spice (if you would prefer to make your own Cajun spice, you will need equal parts of ground coriander, oregano and ground black pepper to double equal parts smoked paprika and crushed chillies)
400g long grain rice (rinsed)
200ml dry white wine
2 tomatoes, peeled and diced
650ml chicken or vegetable stock
Half teaspoon saffron, steeped in warm water
1 tablespoon oil, for cooking

Method

Heat the oil in a saucepan and add the onion, peppers, bacon and chorizo. Cook for a few minutes until lightly browned, then add the chilli, garlic and Cajun spice and cook for a couple more minutes.

Stir in the rice to coat with the spices, then add the wine. After about a minute stir in the tomatoes, stock and saffron (including the steeping liquid). Bring to the boil, then reduce to a simmer. Cover with a lid and cook for about 10 to 12 minutes.

Add the prawn tails, salmon and mussels, replace the lid and cook for 3 minutes. Add the squid and smoked salmon and cook for a further 3 minutes, until the seafood is cooked and the rice is tender. Serve immediately.

Spiced Whitby squid with squid ink rice

Serves 4

Ingredients

400g fresh prepared squid
1 heaped teaspoon ground coriander
1 heaped teaspoon garam masala
Half teaspoon ground cumin
Half teaspoon turmeric
Half teaspoon hot chilli powder
Quarter teaspoon garlic salt
1 dessertspoon plain flour
Oil, for cooking
Sea salt and black pepper, to season
Thai basil, to serve

For the raita
300ml natural yoghurt
Half cucumber, very finely diced
1 tablespoon chopped fresh mint
Half green chilli, very finely chopped
Salt and pepper, to season

For the rice
300g paella rice
Half medium onion, finely diced
1 small fennel, finely diced
1 clove crushed garlic
1 sachet squid ink (available from
The Magpie's Whitby Catch –
www.thewhitbycatch.co.uk)
700ml fish stock
Tablespoon oil, for cooking
Salt and pepper, to season

Method

For the raita
Place the cucumber in kitchen paper and squeeze any excess water out. Mix with the yoghurt, mint, chilli and seasoning, then cover and chill. This can be made the day before.

For the rice
In a large shallow pan, lightly sauté the onion, fennel and garlic in the oil until softened. Add the rice, squid ink and fish stock and stir well. Bring to the boil and reduce the heat to a simmer, stirring often. Cook for approximately 20 to 25 minutes or until the rice is tender and most of the stock has been absorbed.

For the squid
Mix the spices and flour together. Add the squid and evenly coat it in the spice mix.

Heat the oil in a deep pan until it reaches about 175°C (do not fill more than one-third full as the oil will bubble up slightly). Carefully lay the squid into the pan; it will take about 2 minutes to cook (do it in 2 batches to evenly cook the fish). Place onto kitchen paper to remove any excess oil, and season lightly with sea salt and freshly milled black pepper.

To serve
Spoon some of the squid ink rice onto the plates and top with the spiced squid. Serve with the raita and Thai basil.

Traditional Whitby fish & chips

Serves 4

Ingredients

4 fillets fresh cod or haddock (about 180g per fillet or 200g for haddock to allow for the skin)
2kg good frying potatoes
Beef dripping, for frying (or rapeseed oil if you prefer)

For the batter
500g plain flour
200g self-raising flour
Half teaspoon baking powder
1lt (approximately) Bradfield Brewery bitter

Method

Firstly make the batter by sieving the flours into a bowl. Add the baking powder then gradually add the bitter, whisking continuously to avoid any lumps. The batter should be the consistency of single cream (too thick and the batter will be crisp on the outside yet stodgy on the inside). Place in the fridge to rest.

Slowly heat the dripping to approximately 150°C (300°F) in a large pan. The dripping should only come no more than halfway up the pan; any more and you run the risk of overflowing the pan.

Peel and cut the potatoes into thick chips – the thicker the better, as thicker chips absorb less fat. Rinse and pat dry. Carefully add the chips to the fat and cook until soft but still slightly firm. Remove and cool slightly.

Turn up the heat to 175°C (370°F). One at a time, dip the fillets of fish into the batter then gently lay them into the dripping. These should take about 7 to 8 minutes to cook, and the batter should look light, golden and crispy. Remove and place onto kitchen paper to drain.

Next place the chips into the hot fat and cook until crisp and golden. Again place onto kitchen paper to drain.

Serve with a big dish of tartare sauce, lemon wedges, salt and vinegar.

John & Sue

Lucy & Lisa

Richard

Josie

James

Meet the Bradfield Brewery FAMILY

Pete

Paul

Sarah

Aaron

Ashley

154

Simon

Duncs (Steve)

Jackie

Alice

Captain (Stuart)

Graeme

Youth (Lee)

Bradley

Adam

Sam

Henrietta

Jordan

Index

Coley with mussel and potato chowder, 120

Kipper
Kipper kedgeree, 128

Lobster
Lobster carbonara, 130

Monkfish
Monkfish and sausage casserole, 132

Mussels
Coley with mussel and potato chowder, 120
Mussels with Farmers Blonde and pancetta, 134
Seafood jambalaya, 146

Oyster
Rump, Farmers Stout and oyster pie, 114

Pasta
Lobster carbonara, 130

Peas
Baked halibut with pea and ham, 112
Seared local scallops, black pudding, pease pudding and spiced tomato sauce, 116
Scampi wrap with pea guacamole, 144

Pepper
Pan fried turbot with ratatouille, 140
Seafood jambalaya, 146

Pork
Monkfish and sausage casserole, 132

Potato
Seared local scallops, black pudding, pease pudding and spiced tomato sauce, 116
Bread brill fillet with Spanish potatoes, 118
Coley with mussel and potato chowder, 120
Pan fried skate wing with warm pickle salad, 138
Scampi wrap with pea guacamole, 144
Traditional Whitby fish & chips, 150

Prawn
Seafood jambalaya, 146

Rice
Kipper kedgeree, 128
Seafood jambalaya, 146
Spiced Whitby squid with squid ink rice, 148

Salmon
Salmon salsa burger, 142
Seafood jambalaya, 146

Scallops
Seared local scallops, black pudding, pease pudding and spiced tomato sauce, 116

Scampi
Scampi wrap with pea guacamole, 144

Skate
Pakora skate cheeks, 136
Pan fried skate wing with warm pickle salad, 138

Squid
Seafood jambalaya, 146
Spiced Whitby squid with squid ink rice, 148

Tomato
Rump, Farmers Stout and oyster pie, 114
Seared local scallops, black pudding, pease pudding and spiced tomato sauce, 116
Bread brill fillet with Spanish potatoes, 118
Coley with mussel and potato chowder, 120
Hake goujons with BBQ dip, 126
Monkfish and sausage casserole, 132
Mussels with Farmers Blonde and pancetta, 134
Pan fried turbot with ratatouille, 140
Salmon salsa burger, 142
Seafood jambalaya, 146

Turbot
Pan fried turbot with ratatouille, 140

We would like to acknowledge and thank the following people:

Alan Smith who is our (unofficial) building inspector and part-time sampler!

Chris Franklin, initial advisor on the diversification.

Andrew Wall, our equipment supplier from Moeschle (UK).

John Hayward, who assisted in the barn-to-brewery conversion.

Andrew Adams, our stainless fabricator, helping to put the brewing equipment together.

Adam Kay for writing the book, and the rest of the team at RMC Media for putting it all together.

Our loyal and hardworking team of staff – Paul Ward, Pete Jackson, Adam Jubb, Sam Jubb, Simon Walker, Ashely Worsfold, Aaron Worsfold, Bradley Worsfold, Graeme Jagger, Stuart Wragg, Jordan Fletcher, Steven Duncombe, Jackie Helliwell, Alice Webster, Henrietta Burkinshaw, Lee Hinchliffe and Sarah Wasteney.

And finally, all our friends and family, and people who have helped and supported us along the way.

CHEERS!

Produced by: